TENNIS DRILLS
FOR SELF-IMPROVEMENT

TENNIS DRILLS FOR SELF-IMPROVEMENT

edited by Steven Kraft

Ten of the nation's top young tennis coaches offer forty-two favorite drills

UNITED STATES TENNIS ASSOCIATION

INSTRUCTIONAL SERIES

Illustrations by George Janes

DOUBLEDAY & COMPANY, INC.
GARDEN CITY, NEW YORK
1978

Library of Congress Cataloging in Publication Data
Main entry under title:

Tennis drills for self-improvement.

(Instructional series)
1. Tennis. 2. Tennis—Training. I. Kraft,
Steven. II. Janes, George. III. Series.
GV995.T42   796.34'22

ISBN: 0-385-12632-8
Library of Congress Catalog Card Number 77–78516

Contents

Contributors

BOB BAYLISS, U. S. Naval Academy

DAVID BENJAMIN, Princeton University

JUDY DIXON, Yale University

JEFF FRANK, Davidson College

ANNE HILL GOULD, Stanford University

STEVE GRIGGS, Yale University

DOUG MACCURDY, Director of Instruction,
Lawrenceville Tennis Camp

BOB McKINLEY, Trinity University

MARILYN MONTGOMERY RINDFUSS, Trinity University

ALICE TYM, University of Tennessee at Chattanooga

Drills are essential in the development of any tennis player. Somewhere between "hitting" and playing a set or a match, drills add *purpose* to hitting *without the pressure* of match play. Aside from helping a player improve the technique of a given stroke or stroke progression, drills strongly contribute to the development of concentration, timing, and court discipline.

ANNE HILL GOULD
Women's Tennis Coach
Stanford University

Drilling is the key to stroke improvement. Tennis is a game in which improvement is made through constant repetition. Playing sets will test your strokes, but not improve them. On the other hand, drilling—constant repetition—without the pressure of winning or losing the point, game, set, or match is the only way to insure consistency in stroke production.

ROBERT BAYLISS
Head Tennis Coach
U. S. Naval Academy

Editor's Note

Most tennis players restrict their tennis activity to informal rallying and actual set or match play. They neglect a third alternative, which may well be the fastest and surest way toward self-improvement—practicing disciplined drills.

Drills focus on one or more aspects of match play in a controlled context, free of competitive pressure. Through the repetition of one shot or one pattern of shots, the player grooves strokes as well as concentration. Anyone who only rallies and plays retards his or her potential growth as a tennis player.

Tennis Drills for Self-improvement may easily be used in a team practice situation, but unlike other tennis drill books, which are geared only to instructional classes or teams, and which require several players and a bucket of balls, this book is written for use in a normal playing situation, involving one to four players and three to six tennis balls. Also, this book is deliberately written without stroke instruction and without drills for beginners. It is designed with the competent player in mind—one who already knows how to play, but wishes to increase his or her level of skill by practicing specific aspects of the game in a controlled situation.

If you have never drilled before, the best way to get into the drilling habit is to find a compatible partner, perhaps one of your regular opponents, and set aside a specific amount of drill time during each play session. Decide what you most need to work on—crosscourt forehands, down-the-line backhands, overheads, or whatever —and choose the drills that best suit your needs.

Don't be embarrassed to take this book to the court with you so that you can use it as a reference or guide. Again, while it is hoped that the book will be used by teachers and coaches as well as players, it is written primarily for the individual player.

Like actual play, your drill sessions will improve with practice. It may be difficult at first to establish a rhythm with your partner that will perpetuate the drill. Start at a moderate pace and emphasize consistency. Remember that, unless the drill so prescribes, the object is not to hit winners, but to keep the ball in play for as long as possible. Moderate pace will help to insure quality practice sessions.

Because drills are more efficient than match play (more balls are hit in a shorter period of time), you will often find a half-hour drill session more valuable than an hour or more of play. This is a good point to keep in mind when your play time is limited.

Tennis Drills for Self-improvement is really the product of its ten contributors, and I am in great debt to them for their co-operation. My job consisted merely in choosing the most effective drills and providing a readable format. Biographical sketches of the contributors can be found in the final section of the book.

Whether you are an aspiring intermediate player or already a tournament champion, it is hoped that this book will raise your level of tennis skill.

Good luck!

Steven Kraft

Three Rhythms, Three Patterns

Serving aside, three fundamental rhythms may be distinguished in tennis play: groundstroke to groundstroke, groundstroke to volley, and volley to volley. In turn, these three rhythms may be practiced in three basic patterns: down-the-line, crosscourt, and figure 8. The first section of tennis drills focuses on these three rhythms and patterns.

1. GROUNDSTROKE DOWN THE LINE

NUMBER OF PLAYERS: Two.

PURPOSE: To improve steadiness and control by practicing the down-the-line shot that occurs in match play.

THE DRILL: Player A and Player B start at the center of opposite baselines and hit the ball down the line, keeping the ball in play as long as possible. If both players are right-handed, A will hit forehands and B will hit backhands (Diagram 1). After several minutes switch the hitting side, so that A hits backhands and B hits forehands (Diagram 2).

NOTES AND VARIATIONS

1. This drill—and all down-the-line drills—may be run with four players on a court.

2. Set a goal of consecutive hits and keep a running count as you drill. Try for ten, twenty-five, fifty in a row.

3. Count only balls that land between the service line and the baseline (Diagram 3).

4. *Alley Rally*: Hit down the line, aiming to keep every ball within the boundaries of the alley. If you wish, keep the ball between an extended service line and the baseline as well (Diagram 4).

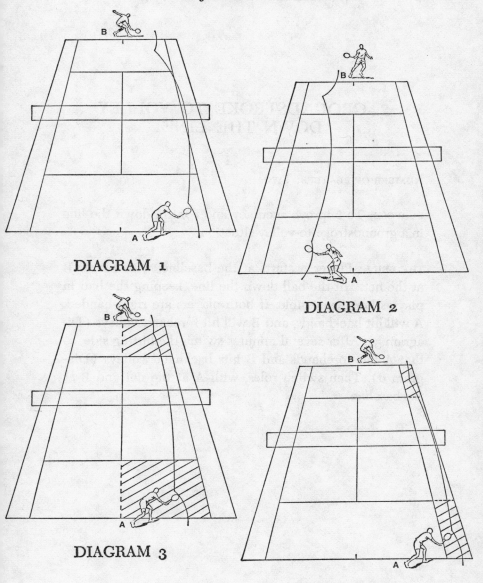

DIAGRAM 1

DIAGRAM 2

DIAGRAM 3

DIAGRAM 4

2. GROUNDSTROKE TO VOLLEY DOWN THE LINE

NUMBER OF PLAYERS: Two.

PURPOSE: To improve accuracy and control down the line in a groundstroke-to-volley situation.

THE DRILL: Player A starts at the baseline, with Player B at the net. Hit the ball down the line, keeping the ball in play as long as possible. If both players are right-handed, A will hit backhands, and B will hit forehand volleys (Diagram 5). After several minutes switch the hitting side, so that A hits forehands and B hits backhand volleys (Diagram 6). Then switch roles, with A at the net and B at the baseline.

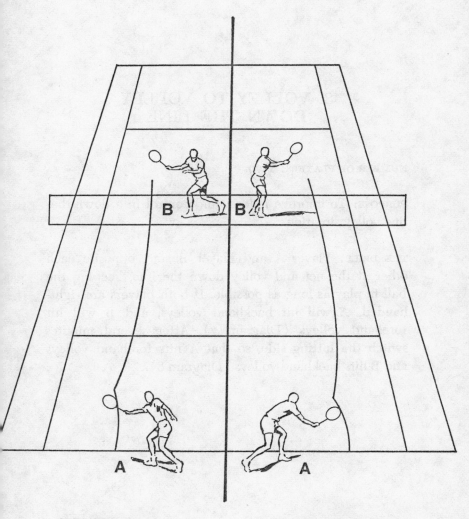

DIAGRAM 5   DIAGRAM 6

3. VOLLEY TO VOLLEY
DOWN THE LINE

NUMBER OF PLAYERS: Two.

PURPOSE: To improve reflexes and control in a down-the-line volley situation.

THE DRILL: Player A and Player B start opposite each other at the net and volley down the line, keeping the ball in play as long as possible. If both players are right-handed, A will hit backhand volleys, and B will hit forehand volleys (Diagram 7). After several minutes switch the hitting side, so that A hits forehand volleys and B hits backhand volleys (Diagram 8).

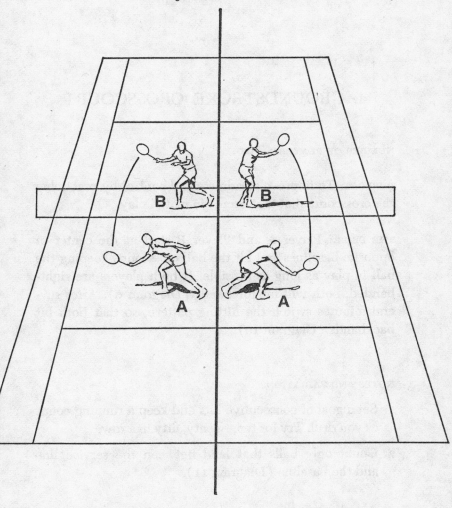

DIAGRAM 7   DIAGRAM 8

4. GROUNDSTROKE CROSSCOURT

NUMBER OF PLAYERS: Two.

PURPOSE: To improve steadiness and control by practicing the crosscourt shot that occurs in match play.

THE DRILL: Player A and Player B start at the center of opposite baselines and hit the ball crosscourt, keeping the ball in play as long as possible. If both players are right-handed, both will hit forehands (Diagram 9). After several minutes switch the hitting pattern, so that both hit backhands (Diagram 10).

NOTES AND VARIATIONS

1. Set a goal of consecutive hits and keep a running count as you drill. Try for ten, twenty, fifty in a row.

2. Count only balls that land between the service line and the baseline (Diagram 11).

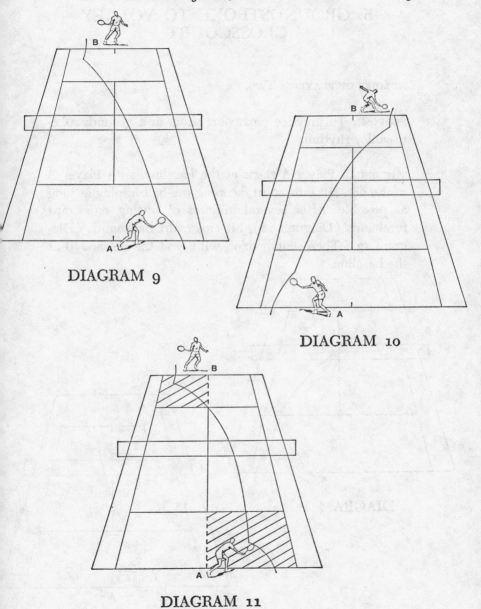

DIAGRAM 9

DIAGRAM 10

DIAGRAM 11

5. GROUNDSTROKE TO VOLLEY
CROSSCOURT

NUMBER OF PLAYERS: Two.

PURPOSE: To practice crosscourt shots in a groundstroke-to-volley rhythm.

THE DRILL: Player A starts at the baseline, with Player B at the net. Hit crosscourt, keeping the ball in play as long as possible. After several minutes of hitting crosscourt forehands (Diagram 12), hit crosscourt backhands (Diagram 13). Then switch roles, with A at the net and B at the baseline.

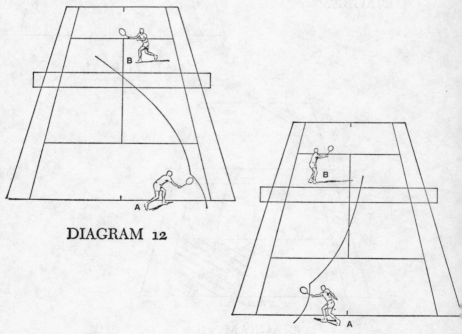

DIAGRAM 12

DIAGRAM 13

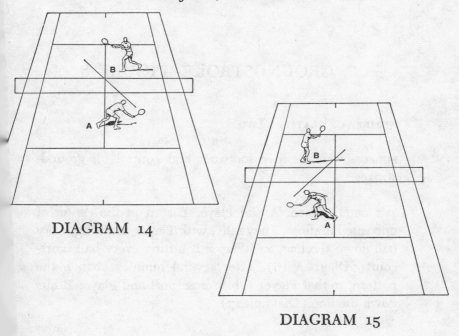

DIAGRAM 14

DIAGRAM 15

6. VOLLEY TO VOLLEY CROSSCOURT

NUMBER OF PLAYERS: Two.

PURPOSE: To improve reflexes and control in a crosscourt volley situation.

THE DRILL: Player A and Player B are positioned opposite each other at the net, and hit the ball crosscourt, keeping the ball in play as long as possible. After several minutes of hitting crosscourt forehand volleys (Diagram 14), switch and hit backhand volleys (Diagram 15).

7. GROUNDSTROKE—FIGURE 8

NUMBER OF PLAYERS: TWO.

PURPOSE: To improve footwork and control on ground-strokes.

THE DRILL: Player A and Player B start at the center of opposite baselines. They rally, with Player A hitting every ball down the line, and Player B hitting every ball cross-court (Diagram 16). After several minutes change the pattern, so that Player A hits crosscourt and Player B hits down the line (Diagram 17).

NOTES AND VARIATIONS

1. Do not discontinue the drill if the pattern is broken. Keep the ball in play while re-establishing the correct pattern.

2. Set a goal of consecutive hits, and keep a running count as you drill.

3. Count only balls that land between the service line and the baseline.

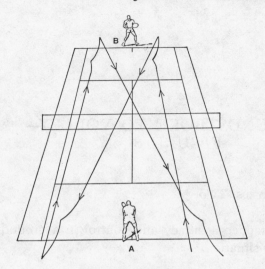

DIAGRAM 16

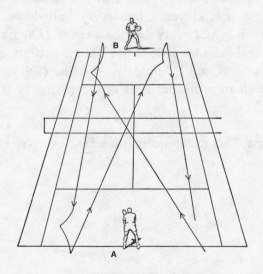

DIAGRAM 17

8. GROUNDSTROKE TO VOLLEY—
FIGURE 8

NUMBER OF PLAYERS: Two.

PURPOSE: To practice accuracy and control in a ground-stroke-to-volley situation.

THE DRILL: Player A starts at the baseline, with Player B at the net. Player A hits every ball down the line, and Player B hits every ball crosscourt (Diagram 18). After several minutes switch the hitting pattern, so that A hits crosscourt and B hits down the line (Diagram 19). Then switch roles so that A is at the net, with B in the backcourt.

NOTE: This drill requires an extreme degree of control.

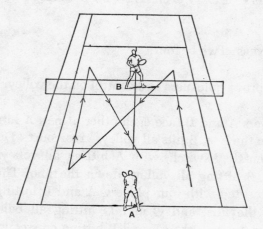

DIAGRAM 18

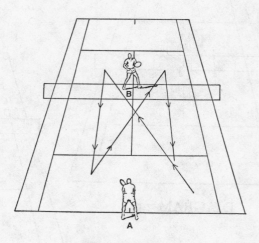

DIAGRAM 19

9. VOLLEY TO VOLLEY—FIGURE 8

NUMBER OF PLAYERS: Two or four.

PURPOSE: To improve quickness and control on the volley.

THE DRILL: Players A and B face each other at net. A hits all volleys down the line, B hits all volleys crosscourt (Diagram 20). Then they switch, with A hitting all volleys crosscourt, and B hitting all volleys down the line. The drill may be executed with four players, A and B hitting all balls down the line, and C and D hitting all balls crosscourt (Diagram 21), then A and B hitting crosscourt and C and D hitting down the line.

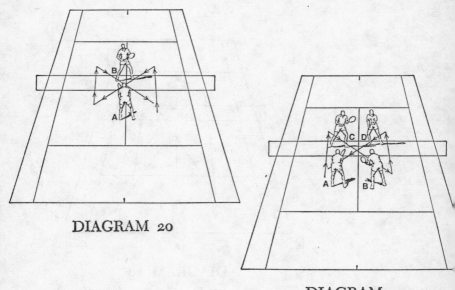

DIAGRAM 20

DIAGRAM 21

Two Additional Groundstroke Drills

10. DEEP BALL

NUMBER OF PLAYERS: Two.

PURPOSE: To increase steadiness and practice achieving depth on groundstrokes.

THE DRILL: Player A and Player B start at the center of opposite baselines. Player A puts the ball into play by bouncing it and hitting a forehand to B. The ball must land behind the service line to be good, and Player A has only one chance for a good "serve." Play continues, with both players aiming to hit the ball behind the service line and within the baselines and singles sidelines (Diagram 22). If a player hits the ball short of the service line or outside the baseline or sidelines, he or she loses the point. Play is to twenty-one, with each player putting the ball into play five times in a row, as in Ping-Pong.

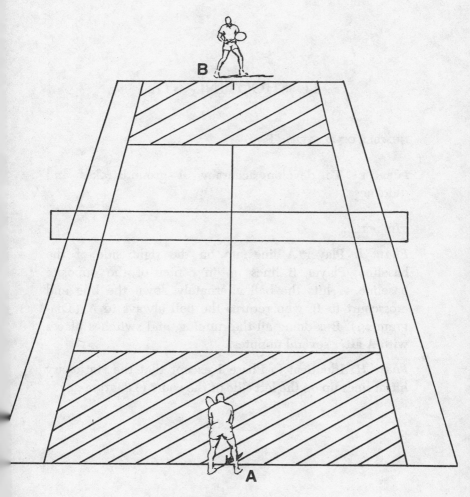

DIAGRAM 22

11. SHOOTING STAR

NUMBER OF PLAYERS: Two.

PURPOSE: To develop accuracy of groundstrokes and quickness.

THE DRILL:

Phase I: Player A lines up on the right side of the baseline. Player B lines up in center of the opposite baseline. A hits the ball alternately down the line and crosscourt to B, who returns the ball always to A (Diagram 23). B is doing all the running, and switches places with A after several minutes.

Phase II: Identical to Phase I except that the stationary hitter lines up on the left side of the court (Diagram 24).

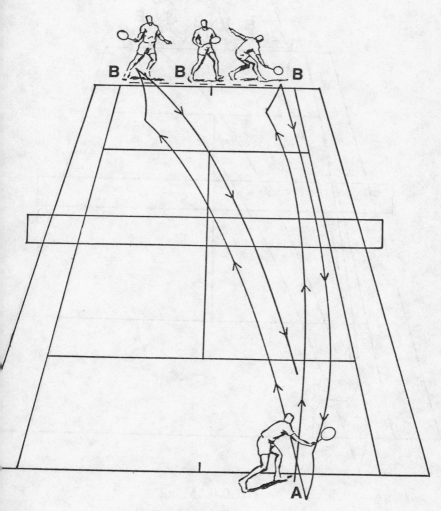

DIAGRAM 23

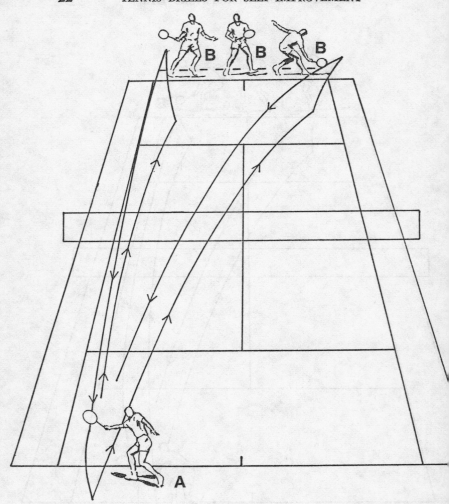

DIAGRAM 24

More
Groundstroke-to-volley
Drills

12. EXHAUSTION

NUMBER OF PLAYERS: Three.

PURPOSE: To improve volley placement, to work on groundstroke footwork.

THE DRILL: Players A and B position themselves at the net. Player C, the primary focus of the drill, starts at the center of the opposite baseline. Players A and B feed balls to Player C that force him to run but are within reach. The point is to run C from side to side and up and back. C must return the balls to A and B. Players switch roles after several minutes (Diagram 25).

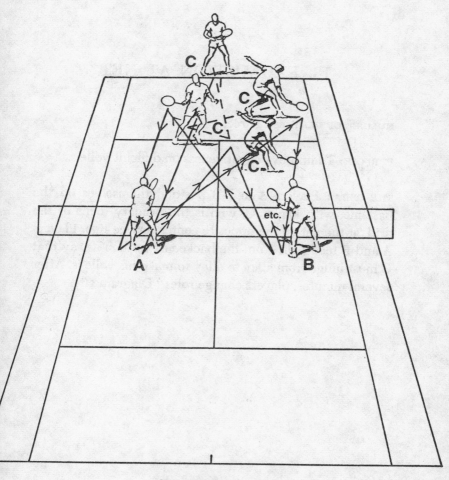

DIAGRAM 25

13. EXHAUSTION AT NET

NUMBER OF PLAYERS: Three.

PURPOSE: To improve effectiveness on difficult volleys.

THE DRILL: Players A and B position themselves on the baseline, with Player C, who is the primary focus of the drill, at the net on the opposite center service line. Players A and B feed balls from the backcourt in such a way that C must lunge from alley to alley to make his volleys. After several minutes, players change roles (Diagram 26).

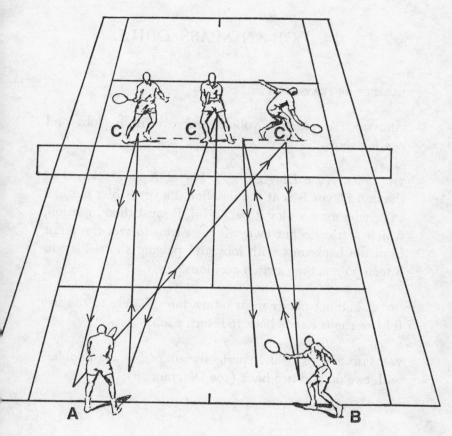

DIAGRAM 26

14. LOB-AND-PASS DRILL

NUMBER OF PLAYERS: Two.

PURPOSE: To practice volleys and overheads, lobs and passing shots.

THE DRILL: (see Diagram 27). Player A is positioned at the net, Player B is at the baseline. Player B hits the ball to A, who must volley it back to B. B must then hit a lob, which A tries to put away. B then tries to win the point from the backcourt with lobs and passing shots. Play to fifteen points, then switch positions.

NOTE: The net player must return immediately to the net if he or she is forced back to return a lob.

VARIATION: This drill is perfectly adaptable for doubles, with two up and two back (see Diagram 28).

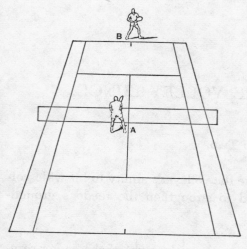

DIAGRAM 27

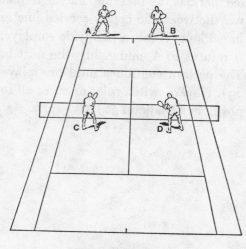

DIAGRAM 28

15. THE VOLLEY LUNGE

NUMBER OF PLAYERS: Two.

PURPOSE: To improve the volleyer's ability to hit wide volleys effectively, and to strengthen the feeder's groundstrokes.

THE DRILL: Player A stands to the right of the center service mark at the baseline. Player B stands at the net, halfway between the center service line and the singles sideline. Player A hits a ball wide to player B down the alley, B returns to A, and A hits the next ball wide crosscourt. The pattern continues until one player misses (Diagram 29). Players switch roles to cover all four possible starting positions (Diagram 30).

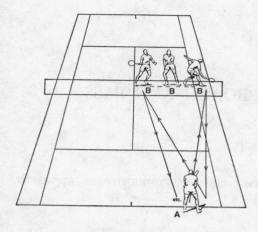

DIAGRAM 29

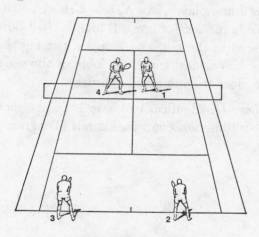

DIAGRAM 30

16. APPROACH AND PASS

NUMBER OF PLAYERS: Two.

PURPOSE: To practice crosscourt groundstrokes, approach shots, and passing shots.

THE DRILL:

Phase I: Players A and B hit deep crosscourt forehands until one player, say A, hits a short ball (one that lands inside the service box). B hits the ball down the line and comes to the net, and A hits a passing shot either down the line or crosscourt. No lobbing allowed (Diagram 31—bounces are numbered in order).

Phase II: Identical to Phase I, except that players begin by hitting crosscourt backhands (Diagram 32).

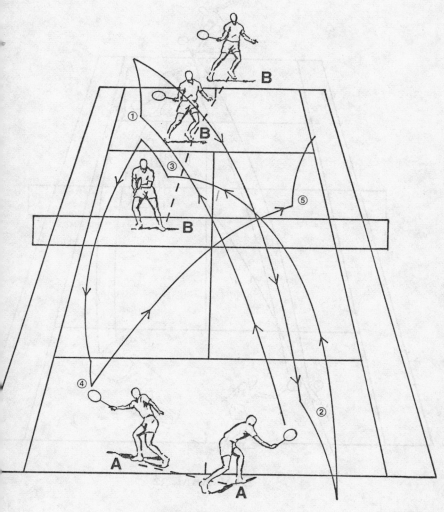

DIAGRAM 31

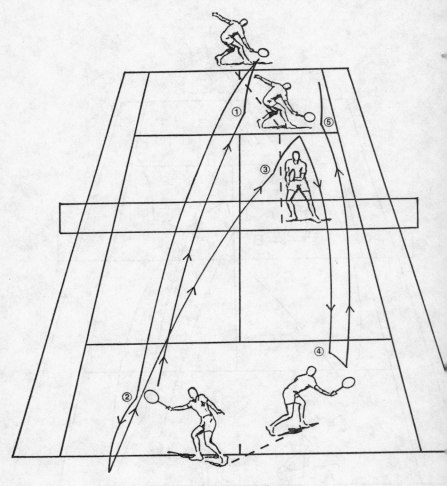

DIAGRAM 32

More Volley Drills

17. CLOSING IN AT NET

NUMBER OF PLAYERS: Two.

PURPOSE: To develop reflexes and volleying skills.

THE DRILL: Players A and B stand on opposite service lines and volley back and forth, moving in to within a yard of the net. In the beginning, hit the ball softly. After several minutes, increase the pace so that the exchange is rapid-fire (Diagram 33).

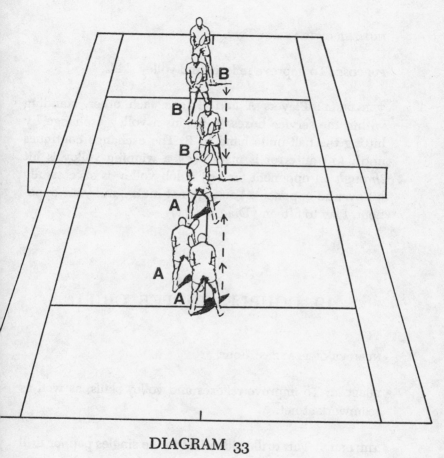

DIAGRAM 33

18. SINGLES PEPPER DRILL

NUMBER OF PLAYERS: Two.

PURPOSE: To improve reflexes and volley skills.

THE DRILL: Players A and B face each other, standing within the service boxes. A begins a volley exchange by hitting the ball underhand to B. The exchange continues until: (1) an error is made, (2) a winning volley is hit *through* an opponent, or (3) a lob volley is successfully hit over an opponent. You may not hit *around* your opponent. Play to fifteen (Diagram 34).

19. DOUBLES PEPPER DRILL

NUMBER OF PLAYERS: Four.

PURPOSE: To improve reflexes and volley skills, as well as teamwork at net.

THE DRILL: This drill is identical to the singles pepper drill except that it involves four people and now angle volleys are permissible. Play to fifteen points.

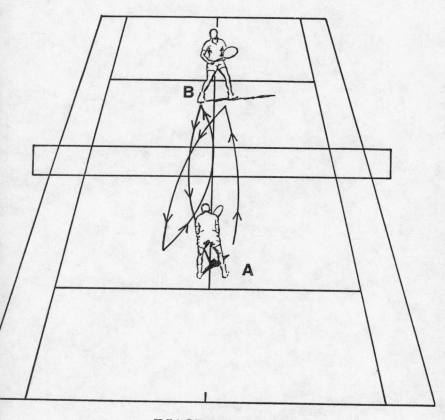

DIAGRAM 34

Drills for Serve
and Return of Serve

20. SERVING PRACTICE

NUMBER OF PLAYERS: One.

PURPOSE: To improve the serve.

NOTES: In practicing the serve, always have a goal in mind. Aim for a target area and/or try for a certain number of good serves in a row.

Set up targets (tennis cans, racket covers, etc.) in various areas of the service court, preferably deep and in the corners. Aim for these.

Serve imaginary games in which you allow yourself two serves in each court. If you make your first serve, serve into the next court. If you miss, serve your second serve.

Serve five minutes to each of the following target areas: (1) the forehand corner of the deuce court, (2) the backhand corner of the deuce court, (3) the forehand corner of the ad court, and (4) the backhand corner of the ad court.

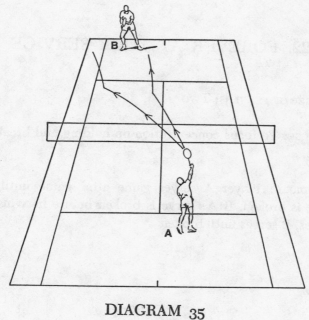

DIAGRAM 35

21. RETURNING THE BIG SERVE

NUMBER OF PLAYERS: Two.

PURPOSE: To quicken reactions to a fast serve.

THE DRILL: Player A serves to Player B from a point mid-way between the service line and the baseline. B must try to react quickly enough to handle the serve (Diagram 35).

22. FOREVER AT YOUR SERVICE

NUMBER OF PLAYERS: Two

PURPOSE: To focus concentration on holding and breaking serve.

THE DRILL: Player A serves game after game until his serve is broken. If A's serve is broken before he wins six games, B serves until broken.

23. ONE TO A CUSTOMER

NUMBER OF PLAYERS: Two or four.

PURPOSE: To improve the consistency and effectiveness of the second serve.

THE DRILL: Play a set—or match—of singles or doubles in which each player is allowed only one serve per point. The point is lost if this serve is missed.

Miscellaneous Drills

24. SIX-BALL PATTERNED SEQUENCE

NUMBER OF PLAYERS: Two.

PURPOSE: To increase concentration and consistency and to spot weaknesses.

THE DRILL: A, the feeder, stands at the baseline, with B at net on the opposite center service line. A feeds B 6 balls in the following sequence: (1) one forehand volley, (2) one backhand volley, (3) one lob over B's head that must be taken on the bounce, (4) one short ball to the forehand for an approach down the line, (5) one backhand volley, and (6) one lob for an overhead. The sequence may be altered to suit specific needs.

NOTE: The feeder should have six balls ready before beginning the drill.

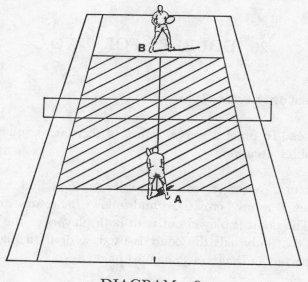

DIAGRAM 36

25. MINITENNIS

NUMBER OF PLAYERS: Two.

PURPOSE: To improve touch, footwork, and movement close to the net.

THE DRILL: Play a set using only the service line and singles sidelines as boundaries. To serve, drop the ball and hit a forehand into the diagonally opposite service court. Switch courts on every serve, as in regular play. *No volleying* (Diagram 36).

26. DOUBLES FOR TWO

NUMBER OF PLAYERS: Two.

PURPOSE: To practice serve, return of serve, and volley in a doubles situation.

THE DRILL: A serves from a doubles position and rushes the net. B returns crosscourt and follows his return to the net. The point is played out with both players at the net. Note that only half the court is used, as if both players had partners (Diagram 37 on next page).

27. HIGH-LOW SIX-BALL SEQUENCE

NUMBER OF PLAYERS: Two.

PURPOSE: To develop control on the volley and overhead and force the player to close in again after an overhead.

THE DRILL: A at the baseline hits six balls to B at the net, alternating low volleys and overheads. Both A and B try to keep the last ball in play as long as possible.

NOTE: The feeder should have six balls ready when the drill begins.

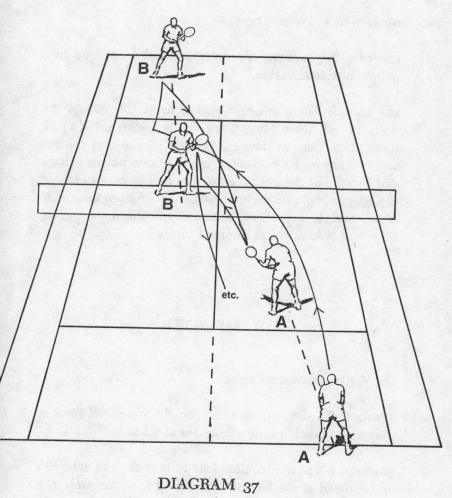

etc.

DIAGRAM 37

28. TWO-ON-ONE DRILLS

NUMBER OF PLAYERS: Three.

PURPOSE: To improve concentration and technique in a unique hitting situation.

THE DRILLS: There are four variations of the two-on-one drill: (1) all three players are in the backcourt, (2) all three players are at the net, (3) one player is at the net and two are in the backcourt, and (4) one player is back and two are at the net. Keeping the ball in play in any of the four configurations improves concentration and technique and is especially valuable for the lone player. Players should rotate at frequent intervals.

29. MURDER

NUMBER OF PLAYERS: Three.

PURPOSE: To develop accuracy on the overhead for one player and quickness of reflexes for another.

THE DRILL: A at the baseline lobs to B at the net, who hits an overhead at the feet of C, standing approximately two feet behind the service line. C attempts to return the overhead (Diagram 38 on next page).

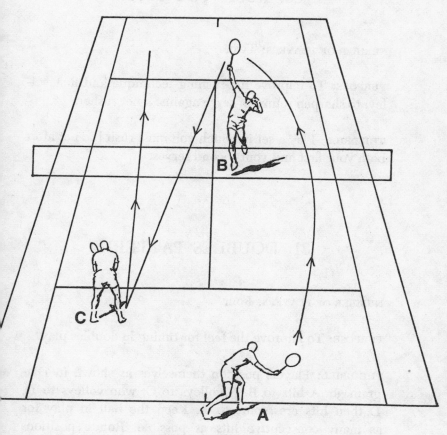

DIAGRAM 38

30. RUSH YOU MUST

NUMBER OF PLAYERS: Two.

PURPOSE: To improve net-rushing technique and first volley; to sharpen return of serve against a net rusher.

THE DRILL: Play a set in which you must rush the net after both your first and your second serves.

31. DOUBLES PATTERN

NUMBER OF PLAYERS: Four

PURPOSE: To improve the feel for timing in doubles play.

THE DRILL: Players position themselves as shown in Diagram 39. A hits to B. B volleys to C, who volleys to D. D then hits crosscourt to A. Keep the ball in play for as many consecutive hits as possible. Rotate positions after several minutes.

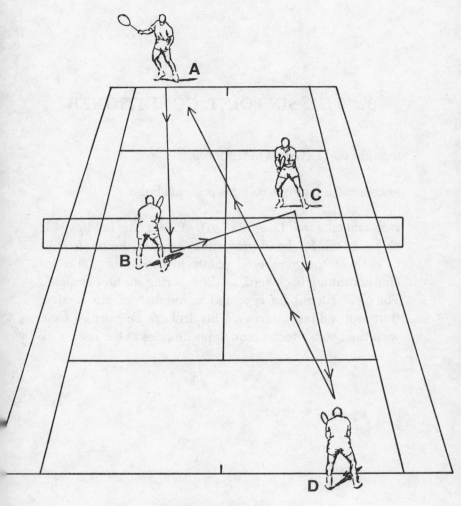

DIAGRAM 39

32. THE SIX-POINT CONDITIONER

NUMBER OF PLAYERS: One or more.

PURPOSE: To improve stamina and quickness.

THE DRILL: (see Diagram 40). Player A, holding his racket in the forehand grip, runs as fast as he or she can to each of the numbered points in succession. This includes running backward, as if preparing for an overhead. The drill should be repeated a number of times after thirty-second rest intervals. This drill can be run as a race, with the two contestants on opposite sides of the net.

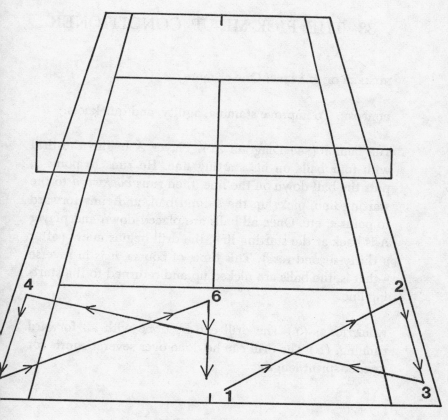

DIAGRAM 40

33. THE PICK-ME-UP CONDITIONER

NUMBER OF PLAYERS: One or more.

PURPOSE: To improve stamina, agility, and quickness.

THE DRILL: (see Diagram 41). Player A begins the drill with four balls on his starting line. He runs to point 1, puts the ball down on the line, then runs *backward* to the starting line, picks up the second ball, and runs forward to point 2, etc. Once all balls are placed down and player A is back at the starting line, the drill begins anew (after a thirty-second rest). This time, of course, it is in reverse —that is, the balls are picked up and returned to the starting line.

VARIATIONS: (1) The drill can be done with all forward running. (2) The drill can be done over several courts for greater sprint length.

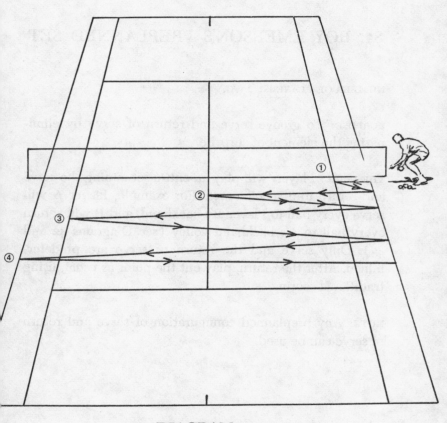

DIAGRAM 41

34. ROY EMERSON'S PREPLANNED SET

NUMBER OF PLAYERS: Two.

PURPOSE: To groove serve and return of serve by eliminating the element of surprise.

THE DRILL: Players will play an entire set aiming the serve and return to a specific area. For example, Player A will serve every ball to Player B's backhand, and B will return every ball to A's backhand volley (see Diagrams 42 and 43). Only serve and the return of serve are predetermined. After the return, play out the point as usual, using traditional scoring.

NOTE: Any preplanned configuration of serve and return of serve can be used.

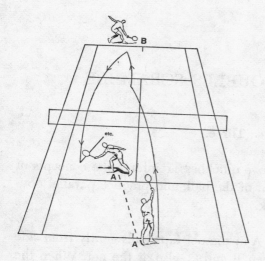

DIAGRAM 42

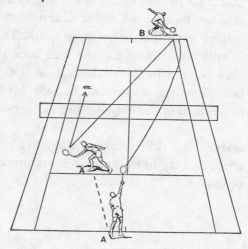

DIAGRAM 43

35. DOUBLES SCRAMBLE

NUMBER OF PLAYERS: Three.

PURPOSE: To improve quickness, reinforce the concepts of following the flight of the ball, and practice parallel doubles and teamwork.

THE DRILL: Player A at the net taps balls gently from side to side and between B and C, also at the net. When the ball is hit to the right, both B and C must move right and attempt to keep an equal distance apart. B and C must call for each shot in between them. They are not allowed to volley and must tap the ball back gently to A. A may also lob the ball, in which case both players must run back together, let the ball bounce, hit the shot back to A, and return to the net together (Diagram 44).

NOTE: This drill is exhausting. Start with a one-minute effort and try to increase your endurance to three minutes or longer.

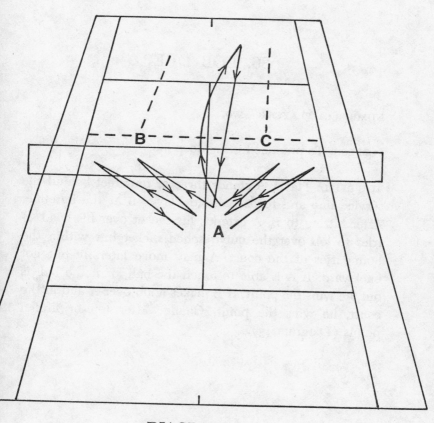

DIAGRAM 44

36. LOB DEEP

NUMBER OF PLAYERS: Two.

PURPOSE: To practice hitting deep lobs.

THE DRILL: Player A stands three or four feet behind the service line and feeds balls to Player B at the baseline. After hitting to B, A extends his racket over his head. B tries to lob over the outstretched racket but within the boundaries of the court. A may move laterally but not backward. If A is able to touch the ball, or if the ball is out, he wins the point. If B makes a lob over A and in the court, he wins the point. Change after ten or fifteen points (Diagram 45).

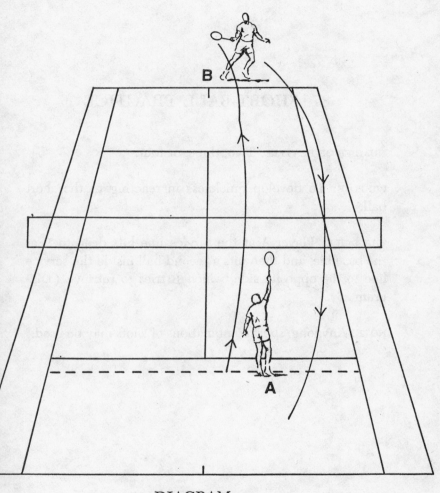

DIAGRAM 45

37. SHORT-BALL PRACTICE

NUMBER OF PLAYERS: Two, three, or four.

PURPOSE: To develop quickness in reacting to the short ball.

THE DRILL: Player A at the service line hits deep to B at the baseline, and then hits a second ball inside the service line to the opposite side, which B tries to retrieve (Diagram 46).

NOTE: Any long/short combinations of shots may be used.

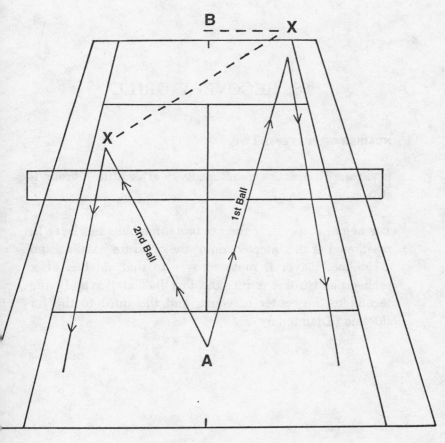

DIAGRAM 46

38. RECOVERY DRILL

NUMBER OF PLAYERS: Two.

PURPOSE: To practice quick recovery after hitting ground-strokes.

THE DRILL: Player A at the net hits three balls to Player B, positioned at the intersection of the opposite baseline and a sideline. Player B must recover to that sideline after each groundstroke. A hits the first ball at Player B, the second to the center of court, and the third to the far sideline (Diagram 47).

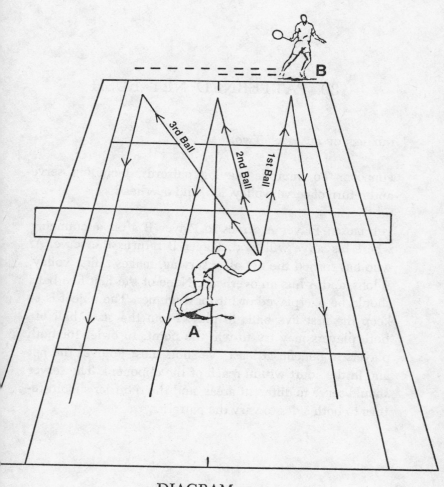

DIAGRAM 47

39. PATTERNED NET RUSH

NUMBER OF PLAYERS: Two.

PURPOSE: To improve playing patterns, including serve and return of serve, volley, lob, and overhead.

THE DRILL: Player A serves to Player B after announcing where his serve will land. Player B returns the serve. A, who has rushed the net after serving, makes a first volley, B lobs, and A hits an overhead. None of the first five balls should be overplayed or hit for a winner. The object is to keep the first five balls in play. From the sixth ball on, both players may try to win the point. In order for both players to benefit, at least five shots must go over the net and in the court within reach of the opponent. The server should serve to different areas, and the returner should return to both sides to vary the pattern.

40. AUSSIE GAME

NUMBER OF PLAYERS: TWO.

PURPOSE: To practice topspin passing shots. Player B on the baseline must hit dipping topspin shots to win. If he hits underspin, the net man, A, will be able to volley offensively.

THE DRILL: The game is played to eleven points. Only half the court, including the alleys, is used. Player A stands in normal volleying position halfway between the service line and the net. Player B stands on the baseline. B always begins by hitting a medium-speed ball to A, who volleys it back without trying to put the ball away. The first two shots don't count. Beginning with the third shot, both players try to win the point, B with a passing shot, A with an offensive volley. No lobbing is allowed. After one game is completed, A and B change places and play again.

41. HALF-COURT SCRAMBLE

NUMBER OF PLAYERS: Two.

PURPOSE: To improve footwork. The drill forces Player B to change direction and sprint short distances many times in the space of a minute, simulating match-play footwork.

THE DRILL: Player A stands a racket-and-arm's length from the net. Player B stands on the service line. A hits soft-angle volleys, forcing B to run as much as possible; B must tap the ball right back to A. If a ball is missed, A feeds the next one from his hand. B's running should be continuous. The drill should last about a minute (Diagram 48).

NOTE: A sample series of shots is given in the diagram. A's volleys make B run from position P_1 to P_2 to P_3 to P_4, with B always hitting directly to A.

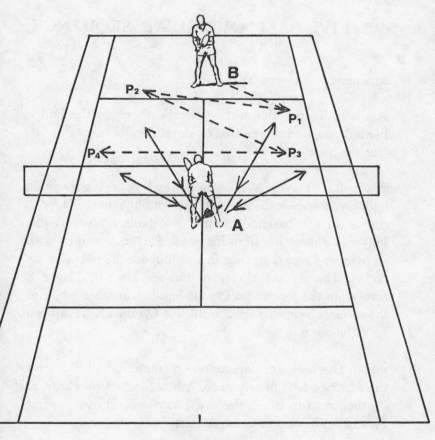

DIAGRAM 48

42. FIVE-BALL OVERHEAD SEQUENCE

NUMBER OF PLAYERS: Two.

PURPOSE: To practice hitting overheads when the ball is behind you, and to practice closing in on the net after hitting the overhead.

THE DRILL: Player A takes a normal volleying position halfway between the service line and the net. Player B stands on the baseline holding five balls. Player B hits Player A a deep lob from his hand. Player A returns with an overhead and then runs in and touches the net with his racket. The instant Player A touches the net, Player B throws up the second ball in his hand as another lob, and the sequence repeats itself until five overheads have been hit (Diagram 49).

NOTE: The diagram depicts one of many possibilities for the first two lobs in sequence. A hits the first overhead at P_1, then runs to touch the net, hits a second overhead at P_2, and again runs to touch the net.

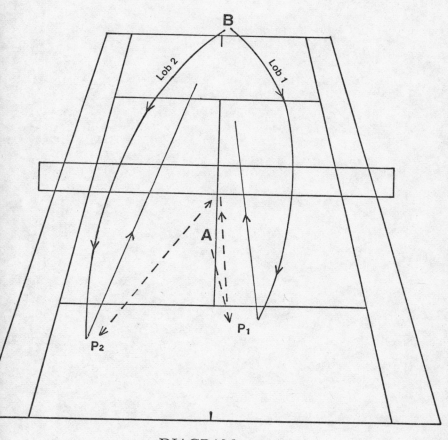

DIAGRAM 49

Contributors

BOB BAYLISS, head tennis coach at Navy, has turned that school's previously mediocre tennis program into one of the finest in the East. In six seasons he has compiled a 125–42 won-lost record.

A graduate of the University of Richmond, where he captained the tennis team during his senior year, Bob has held a high ranking in the Middle Atlantic Tennis Association. He has served as president of the Eastern Intercollegiate Tennis Association, and is a member of the USPTA. He has also served on the USTA national ranking committee for the junior and boys' divisions.

Bob and his wife, Patricia, have three young children, a daughter and two sons.

DAVID BENJAMIN, former Harvard University tennis captain and a leading member of Harvard's national championship squash team, is now director of racquet sports and coach of the men's varsity tennis and squash teams at Princeton University.

David was ranked as a junior by the Eastern Lawn Tennis Association from 1958 to 1963 and played in the qualifying round of the national championships at Forest Hills in 1963.

Elected to Phi Beta Kappa at Harvard, and a finalist in the Rhodes Scholarship competition, David graduated magna cum laude in 1966 and received a Charles Henry Fiske Fellowship for study at Trinity College in Cambridge, England. He received his M.A. degree from Trinity in 1968, graduating with honors. He began his doctoral studies in American civilization at Harvard at 1968, and is presently finishing his Ph.D. requirements.

Aside from tennis teaching stints at various clubs in the United States, David has taught the national team of Togo in western Africa and was director of the International Tennis-Ski Camp in St. Moritz, Switzerland.

David and his wife, Martine, have a young son, Alexander.

JUDY DIXON, a 1972 graduate of the University of Southern California, is currently the field promotion manager of Bancroft Sporting Goods.

Her playing career has been outstanding. In 1967 she partnered with Billie Jean King in the Women's National Indoor Championships and was runner-up in this event. In the same year she won the Junior National Indoors in singles. Three times Judy has been ranked in the East in her junior division.

As impressive as her playing record is her record as a tennis sportscaster on television. With Bud Collins, she has worked at the Canadian Open Championships and the U. S. Clay Court Championships. She has announced countless World Team Tennis telecasts, and she is the first woman ever to be nominated as a sportscaster for an Emmy Award.

Judy's non-tennis interests include music, downhill and cross-country skiing, swimming, sailing, riding, and interior decorating.

JEFF FRANK, who holds a law degree from the University of Florida, is the highly successful tennis coach at Davidson College and director of the Davidson College Tennis Camp. Jeff's five-year coaching record is 98 and 38.

Jeff has taught tennis for many years at camps and

clubs, and has served as a USTA clinician at various conferences. While in law school he helped coach the University of Florida team to two SEC titles, and a Number 5 national ranking.

In 1973 and 1974 Jeff was tournament director for the Boys 14 National Championships. Now he is on two USTA committees and three in the SLTA. In 1975 he was named Southern Conference Coach of the Year in tennis.

ANNE HILL GOULD, who was graduated from Stanford University in 1971, is now the women's tennis coach at Stanford. In her first year of coaching, Anne's team earned second place in the USTA National Intercollegiates, as they finished just one point behind Trinity. Last year they finished second to USC in the AIAW Nationals.

Anne was ranked Number 1 in both the junior and women's divisions in Venezuela in 1968, and has played in the Orange Bowl and Junior Wimbledon.

STEVE GRIGGS, for several years a modern language teacher and tennis coach at the secondary school level on both the East and West coasts, is now the tennis coach at Yale University.

Steve grew up in Ojai, California, and then went east to Trinity College in Hartford, Connecticut, where he captained the tennis team. He also played squash and soccer, for which he was named to the All-New England team in 1966.

Aside from teaching tennis at various clubs, Steve has been a staff member of Tony Trabert's camp in California and also at several soccer camps. In the summer of 1976 he was director of the Steve Griggs' Scandinavian/ American Tennis Program in Finland and Sweden. In 1977 he was pro at the Nantucket Yacht Club.

In the ranking for 1976 Griggs was eighth in New England men's singles and third in doubles.

In his second year as coach at Yale, Griggs took his team to the final 16 in the National Championships. The overall record for 1977 was 16–5.

STEVE KRAFT (editor) is coordinator of junior affairs for the United States Tennis Association and administrator of the USTA International Tennis Teaching Project.

Steve graduated from Harvard University, where he was elected to Phi Beta Kappa, and won the Deturs Prize for academic record.

Three times ranked Number 1 in his age division by the Middle States Tennis Association, Steve's tennis accomplishments include two junior doubles titles—one sectional and one national (Canadian)—with partner Dick Stockton.

A frequent contributor to *Tennis USA*, Steve is co-author with Connie Haynes of the forthcoming Doubleday book, *The Tennis Player's Diet*.

DOUG MACCURDY, a top clinician for the USTA National Tennis Development Program, is a tennis professional with a broad range of tennis experience. He has directed tennis camps and programs at many locations around the United States. He was director of TennisAmerica Touring Camp, the Laver-Emerson Adult Tennis Camp, and currently directs the Lawrenceville (New Jersey) Tennis Camp.

Doug has also worked extensively with the Princeton Community Tennis Program.

In 1975–76 Doug traveled to Indonesia and Malaysia for three months as a tennis clinician for the USTA International Tennis Teaching Project. In 1977 he held three months of workshops throughout Mexico.

BOB McKINLEY, a member of Trinity University's 1972 NCAA championship team, is now director of tennis and men's tennis coach at Trinity.

For four years, from 1969 to 1972, Bob was an NCAA All-American. He was National Junior Champion in 1968 and has won seven other national championships (including the National Junior Indoor singles and doubles and the U. S. Amateur doubles titles).

At the NCAA tournament in 1972, Bob was voted the Rafael Osuna Award recognizing sportsmanship, contributions to tennis, and outstanding ability.

Ranked among the top twenty in U.S. men's tennis for four years, Bob left the professional circuit to become director of tennis at Trinity in December 1973. In three years as head coach, Bob has compiled a record of sixty-eight wins and ten losses. He was named the NCAA tennis Coach of the Year in 1977, while leading his team to a second place finish. Bob was also named to coach the United States team in the World University Games in Sofia, Bulgaria, in August of 1977.

Coach McKinley is the director and chief instructor at Trinity's "Home of the Champions" Summer Tennis Camp, now in its fifth year of operation.

Bob and his wife, Elaine, have two children, Sean and Shannon.

MARILYN MONTGOMERY RINDFUSS, a 1957 Trinity University honor graduate who was ranked seventh in the United States in 1961, and coached the National Junior Wightman Cup Team for seven years, is currently the coach of the Trinity women's tennis team.

Marilyn was ranked among the top twenty in U.S. women's tennis for four years. In 1960 she achieved her highest ranking in doubles, fifth in the nation with Linda Vail, now Mrs. Dennis Van der Meer.

Marilyn received the Marlboro Award for services to tennis in 1963, but her proudest achievement came in the same year when she was awarded the Service Bowl as "the player who yearly makes the most notable contribution to the sportsmanship, fellowship and service of tennis."

From 1961 through 1968, with a one-year break that allowed her to earn her master's degree in mathematics at Louisiana State University, Marilyn coached the National Junior Wightman Cup Team.

For the past eleven years, Marilyn has taught mathematics at San Antonio College, where she holds a rank of associate professor. She recently resigned her teaching duties there in order to coach full time at Trinity.

Most of Marilyn's outside interests center around her family and a wide variety of pets, but she is also an excellent bowler and water skier.

ALICE TYM is the coach of the women's tennis team at the University of Tennessee at Chattanooga. A graduate of the University of Florida where she was Number 1 and captain of the tennis team for four years, Alice has been ranked Number 1 in the USTA Western section and Number 19 and Number 16 among ranked U.S. women.

Alice was elected Southern Tennis Professional of the Year in 1975.

Her extracurricular activities include membership in nature societies, whitewater kyack racing, whitewater canoeing, skiing, and raising fruit trees.

With the co-operation of the United States Tennis Association, Doubleday has published the following titles in this series:

SPEED, STRENGTH, AND STAMINA: Conditioning for Tennis by Connie Haynes with Eve Kraft and John Conroy
Detailed descriptions of exercises for tennis players, and suggestions for keeping in shape.

TACTICS IN WOMEN'S SINGLES, DOUBLES, AND MIXED DOUBLES, by Rex Lardner
A book for women tennis players, with specific suggestions for taking advantage of opponents' weaknesses.

SINISTER TENNIS, by Peter Schwed
How to play against left-handers, and also with left-handers as doubles partners.

RETURNING THE SERVE INTELLIGENTLY, by Sterling Lord
How you can reduce errors, minimize the server's advantage, and launch your own attack.

COVERING THE COURT, by Edward T. Chase
How to be a winning court coverer and keep maximum pressure on your opponent.

THE SERVE AND THE OVERHEAD SMASH, by Peter Schwed
How the intermediate player can best hit the big shots.

FINDING AND EXPLOITING YOUR OPPONENT'S WEAKNESSES, by Rex Lardner

THE VOLLEY AND THE HALF-VOLLEY: The Attacking Game, by John F. Kenfield

TENNIS DRILLS FOR SELF-IMPROVEMENT, edited by Steven Kraft, USTA Education and Research Center
Ten of the nation's top young tennis coaches offer forty-two favorite drills.

The following titles are in preparation:
GROUND STROKES
THE TENNIS PLAYER'S DIET
SPECIALIZATION IN SINGLES, DOUBLES, AND MIXED DOUBLES